Frogs and Toads

FIRST EDITION
DK LONDON: Series Editor Deborah Lock; **Project Editor** Camilla Gersh;
US Senior Editor Shannon Beatty; **Art Director** Martin Wilson;
Producer, Pre-Production Francesca Wardell; **Jacket Designer** Martin Wilson
DK DELHI: Editor Nandini Gupta; **Art Editor** Jyotsna Julka;
DTP Designers Anita Yadav, Syed Md Farhan; **Picture Researcher** Deepak Negi;
Deputy Managing Editor Soma Chowdhury; **Reading Consultant** Linda Gambrell, PhD;
Subject Consultants Dr. Victoria Ogilvy and Sam Taylor, Froglife

THIS EDITION
Editorial Management by Oriel Square
Produced for DK by WonderLab Group LLC
Jennifer Emmett, Erica Green, Kate Hale, *Founders*

Editors Grace Hill Smith, Libby Romero, Michaela Weglinski;
Photography Editors Kelley Miller, Annette Kiesow, Nicole DiMella;
Managing Editor Rachel Houghton; **Designers** Project Design Company; **Researcher** Michelle Harris;
Copy Editor Lori Merritt; **Indexer** Connie Binder; **Proofreader** Larry Shea;
Reading Specialist Dr. Jennifer Albro; **Curriculum Specialist** Elaine Larson

Published in the United States by DK Publishing
1745 Broadway, 20th Floor, New York, NY 10019

Copyright © 2023 Dorling Kindersley Limited
DK, a Division of Penguin Random House LLC
23 24 25 26 10 9 8 7 6 5 4 3 2 1
001-333930-June/2023

A catalog record for this book
is available from the Library of Congress.
HC ISBN: 978-0-7440-7274-7
PB ISBN: 978-0-7440-7275-4

DK books are available at special discounts when purchased in bulk for sales promotions, premiums,
fundraising, or educational use. For details, contact: DK Publishing Special Markets,
1745 Broadway, 20th Floor, New York, NY 10019
SpecialSales@dk.com

Printed and bound in China

The publisher would like to thank the following for their kind permission to reproduce their images:
a=above; c=center; b=below; l=left; r=right; t=top; b/g=background

Alamy Stock Photo: Emanuel Tanjala 16-17; Dorling Kindersley: Peter Janzen 7tr;
Dreamstime.com: Olga Chalovskaia 14cra, Dirk Ercken 14tl; **Getty Images / iStock:** Azureus70 14cl;
naturepl.com: Christian Ziegler 4-5; **Science Photo Library:** Nature Picture Library / MYN / Seth Patterson 12c;
Shutterstock.com: PetlinDmitry 10tr

Cover images: *Front:* **Dreamstime.com:** Hotshotsworldwide c; **Shutterstock.com:** Eroshka cra, Morphart Creation cl;
Spine: **Dreamstime.com:** Hotshotsworldwide

All other images © Dorling Kindersley
For more information see: www.dkimages.com

For the curious
www.dk.com

Frogs and Toads

Karen Wallace

Contents

Meeting Frogs and Toads

Here come the frogs and toads! Frogs have smooth skin and long hind legs. Toads have bumpy skin and short hind legs.

CROAK!

eardrum

Bullfrogs

Bullfrogs make very deep sounds like bulls.

mouth

CROAK!

Mantellas

Mantella frogs come in many colors—black, blue, orange, yellow, or green.

orange

blue

green

yellow

black

Burrowing Toads

Burrowing toads dig holes with their back feet. Their back feet are shaped like spades.

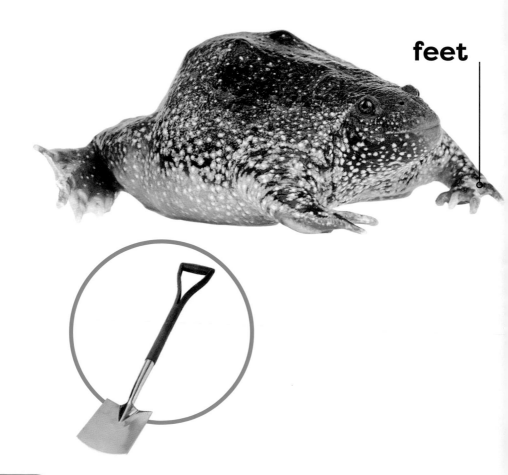

feet

Poison Dart Frogs

Poison dart frogs have poison in their skin. Their skin has bright colors to warn other animals not to eat them.

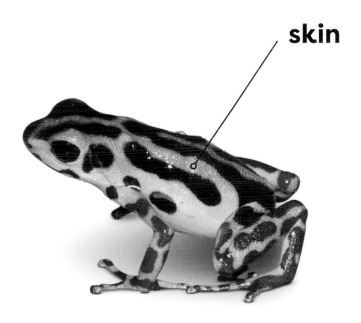

skin

bumpy skin

Cane Toads

Cane toads are some of the biggest toads in the world.

Tree Frogs

Tree frogs can be tiny. They live and hide in trees.

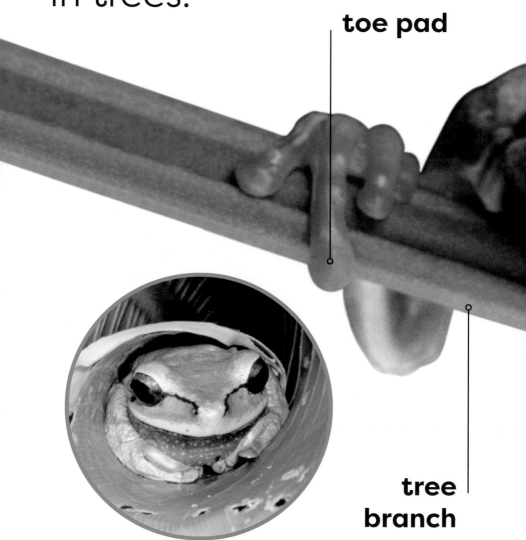

toe pad

tree branch

Fire-Bellied Toads

Fire-bellied toads have bright bellies that scare animals away. Their spots help them hide.

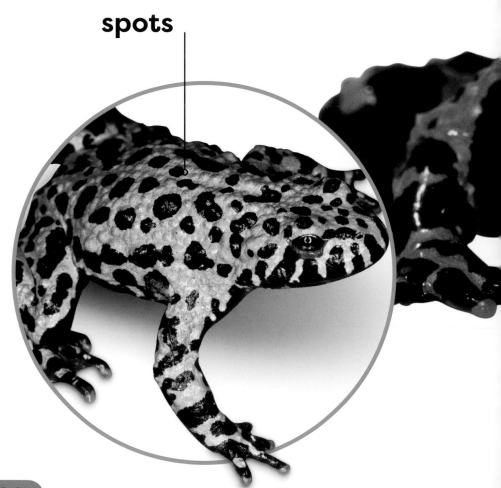

spots

belly

Glass Frogs

The skin of glass frogs can be seen through, like glass.

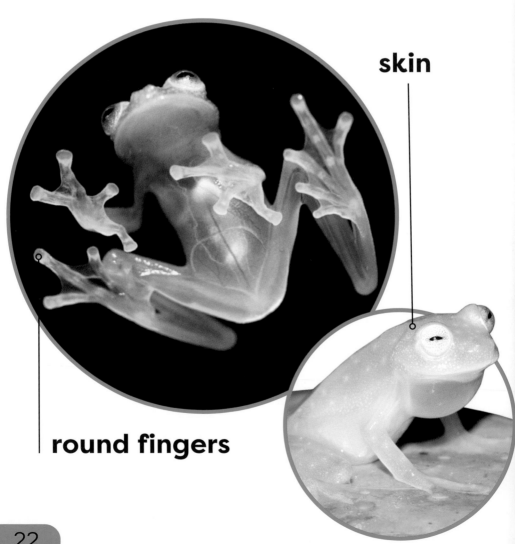

skin

round fingers

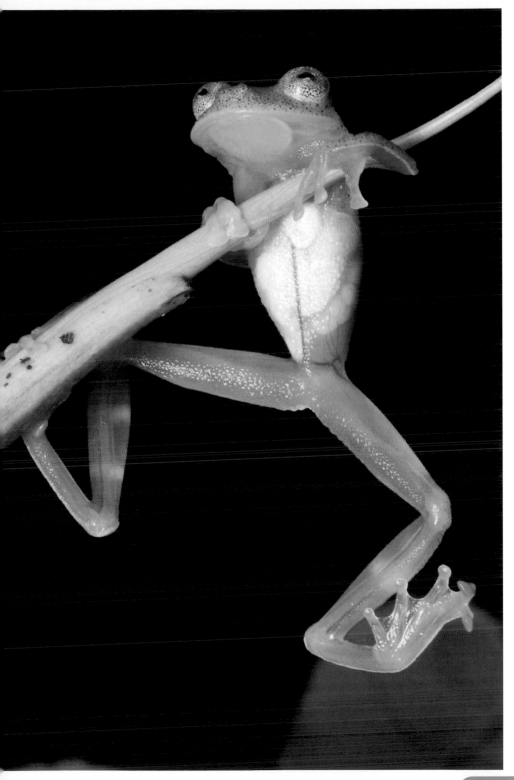

Clawed Frogs

Some frogs have round fingers. Clawed frogs have pointed claws.

claws

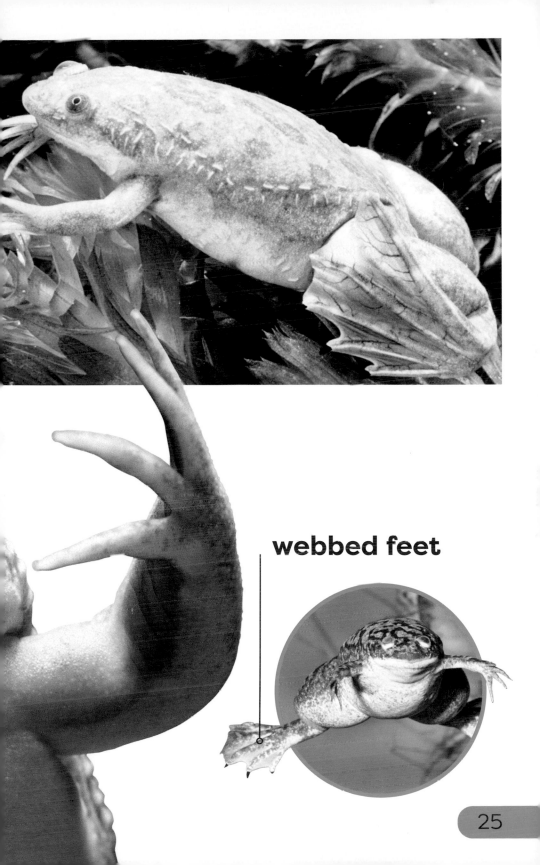

webbed feet

Horned Frogs

Horned frogs have horns that look like big, pointed eyebrows.

horn

Jumping Away

The frogs and toads jump away.

Off they go!

Croak!

Glossary

burrow
the hole where an animal lives

claw
a pointed nail some animals have on their fingers

frog
an animal with slimy skin and long hind legs

horns
points on an animal's head

toad
an animal with dry, bumpy skin and short hind legs

Index

Quiz

Answer the questions to see what you have learned. Check your answers with an adult.

1. What kind of toad digs holes with its back feet?

2. What kind of toad is one of the biggest in the world?

3. How does a fire-bellied toad's bright belly keep the toad safe?

4. What kind of frog has see-through skin?

5. Draw a picture of your favorite frog or toad.

1. A burrowing toad 2. A cane toad 3. By scaring animals away
4. A glass frog 5. Answers will vary